Signature
Author Edition

Signature

-Majestic Forte-
Marcus Yates Ford

Copyright © 2020 Marcus Yates Ford
Majestic Forte All rights reserved. No part of this book may be reproduced, stored in a retrieval system or transmitted in any form or by any means without the prior written permission of the publishers, except by reviewer who may quote brief passages in a review to be printed in a newspaper, magazine, or journal

ISBN-13: 9780578701561
Published by: Majestic Forte
Cover Concept by Marcus Yates Ford
The MF Signature
Houston, Texas
Printed in the United States

Dedication

Seven the number of Completion

Signature

Create Enhance Inspire

The Mind, The Pen, The Paper:
Reflections of the Soul

Love, Grace, and Imani

Freedom of the Mind: Open the Mic

Discovering Devotion

Inspirations

Foundation

Signature

Table of Contents

Signature
Seal 18-19
Signet 20-21
Signature 22
Symbol 23-24
Significance 25-26
Sailboat 27-28
Surrender 29-32

Foundation
Abundant Beauty from the Cross 36
Deeper than what you see 37
Enhancement 38-39
God made me 40
Love is Easy 41
Strings in my Heart 42
The Spirit of Sam/Sam Made me Smile 43
Fallback 44
Looking Back on Vanity 45
Winter Breeze 46
Spiritual Message on My Wrist 47
Zenith 48

Inspirations
The Prelude: The Pulpit 52
Victory 53
Name Above All Names 54-55
This is your Life 56
I Chose 57
The Lamp 58
May Peace be with you 59
A Connoisseur's Limited Release 60

Discovering Devotion

All Eyes on You 64
In My Heart 65
Boarding Pass Please 66-67
Savior & Stars 68-69
The Wishing Well 70
The Crowd of My Thoughts 71
Volume II of my Life 72-73
The MF Signature 74
Love Me (Prelude to Love) 75
Dangerous (My Imagination) 76-77
Cycle 78
Forever & a Day 79
Stars and Entrapment 80
Revamp 81
Tranquility 82-83
Bonfire 84
Unselfish 85
The Afterthought (Epilogue) 86
My Greatest Work 87
When Everything is Meant to be Broken 88-89
Higher Calling 90
The Creativity I make 91-92
Prayer 93
"The After Day" 94-95
Pray 96

The Freedom of the Mind:
First Stage (I Recite) 100-101
September 10th 102-103
The Scion 104-105
The Blueprint 106-107
Confusion 108
Creation 109-1110
Request 111
500 112

Love, Grace and Imani
Who am I? 116
Life's Lessons 117
My Time of Need 118
Moments 119
Him 120
My Downfall, My Demise 121
Send a Lady 122-123
Speak to my Heart 124
Gifts of Grace 125
Still Here 126

The Mind, The Pen, The Paper Reflections of the Soul
The Mind, the Pen, The Paper 130
Wounds 131
Trouble Man 132
When I was Willing 133
Unstoppable 134
You who kept me Strong 135
Where I'm From 136
Coin 137

Signature
Author Edition

7
Signature
7

2020

Sealed, Signet, Signature, Symbol
Significance, Sailboat, Surrender

MAJESTIC FORTE

MARCUS YATES FORD

Cover Concept by Marcus Yates Ford
Photo & Design by April Reed Mooney
U4U Photography and Graphics

Sealed

When I read
Discovering Devotion's "The After Day"
On many nights I was silently speaking
It feels like I am in a timeless dream
The day after my brother passed,
In my mind I hear his voice of laughter,
Us playing with no ideas of the world beyond,
The innocent times of our childhood
And desires to have fun and to compete,
Whether it was video games
or racing down the street
Making decisions on a board game…
His favorite Monopoly
Park Place or Boardwalk
The After Day brings me so much pain
I do not want to talk
Reflection is I am missing a piece of my heart,
You been with me from the start…
I never thought of "The After Day",
However, the after day is here
We will always be together
A bond of us being brothers is forever,
I smile now because you rest easy…
Lord, I pray that he will always be able to reach me
Let me see his presence in the crowd,
This is my prayer written down,
Which keeps me on the ground,
My foundation the "Rock',
What I promote will not stop,
Which is Love as I give from the heart
Pushing Love to hit its mark

Sealed continued...

With God's grace this is how I start,
Taking this to the next level,
I am still willing and able,
And like Able I will give
YOU my best fruits, I will speak the truth;
I cannot make it without YOU,
Give me the strength, be by my side, let them know
They cannot love too much one part of me,
They should not love only one part of me,
They should not love the way the words read,
They should love that You are a part of me,
The freshness under this seal,
I pull it back to let the world experience this is real,
Only love can cause your heart to heal,
The discovery of this has been tremendous,
70 times x 7; forgiveness
Which is the master key,
To a better you to a better me,
To the highest mountain
To the lowest depth in the sea,
I transfer it to the manuscript,
My soul's purpose is to uplift,
I am only concentrating on the gift,
I am keeping it fresh,
Let me package it up
Let you experience it for yourself,
This illustration is real,
Greatness within these pages,
The last book delivered, signed and sealed

Signet

As I partake in this recipe
Whiskey, Whiskey, Whiskey,
Water, Water, Water,
Sleep
The pain is so deep, even 8 years later
The *Born and Raised Album*
song #10 is on repeat
As I open the Glenmorangie Signet,
It becomes the scotch I prefer
I relax and the melody is heard
Two more drinks? Do I need to be asked?
Hard to turndown Glenfiddich Grand Cru
It's 23 years old in a Cuvee Cask
So, I pour into my empty glass, nice and neat
Next round, I even find myself experimenting
With bourbon Eddie Russell's
A Master's Keep
Lord, help me,
give me the strength to gain control
As I feel out of control
As I try to get back to the *Beginnings,*
Saturday in the Park
25 or 6 to 4, it is starting to get dark
It's a *Hard Habit to Break*, I'm a *Street Player*
Hard to Say I'm Sorry
but *Love me Tomorrow*
You're the Inspiration, Make me Smile
As I put the glass down...
Listening to the Geneva Lab
that crystal-clear sound
I been doing this for quite a while

Signet continued

Does Anybody Really Know What Time It Is?
Take Me Back to Chicago
So I can feel the wind, you are *Alive Again*
Silently inside I still weep…
these songs are for LC

I use these seven steps,
now my mission is complete
Whiskey,
Whiskey,
Whiskey,
Water,
Water,
Water,
Sleep

See Page 144

Signature

Signature Smile
Signature Dial
Signature 12
Signature Yell
Signature Mail
Signature Story to Tell
Signature 7

Signature Wish Signature Gift
Signature Phrase Signature Praise
Signature Song Signature Prayer

Signature Cause Signature Cross
Signature Love Signature Dove
Signature Message

Signature Lesson Signature Blessing
Signature 6 Signature Victory

Signature Sapphire Signature Necklace
Signature Bracelet

Signature Trilogy Signature Book

Signature Symbol

Symbol

From the days riding in passenger seat
In the blue beamer with the hammer wheels,
I looked to the stars at night
And ask myself is this real?
I picked up my pen
I wrote my thoughts in my journal,
Gold charm "Je t'aime",
I got exactly what I wanted,
As I laid dormant my dreams
Continue to bounce from heart to heart,
How I have change since I was seventeen,
Now I'm in the white on white 650
with the automatic start,
just a push of the button,
the engine never sounded better as I take a listen,
Some may never understand
What has been mentioned
No jab but now I have my own family
I'm with my queen & my princess,
We walk the shore and reside at Solaz,
I look at the sky at night,
I see the stars so clear,
As I move to the next sentence,
It's another dream that's has my attention
As I'm reminiscing
The Mind, the Pen, the Paper;
Reflections of the Soul,
the MF sign,
The pencil sketch that Ed Thornton designed,
That symbol, how the moments unfold,
Funny how I tried to trap it in a piece of gold,

Symbol continued...

The freedom of a goal,
this is how stories are told,
my poetic flow puts my signature into action,
New pendant, Rose Gold with black karats,
I built this cobblestone
I'm on my "Horse & Carriage"
Chasing this dream to the end of the road
Because the end is closer than
we will ever know,
the caterpillar to a butterfly,
I'm in full growth,
As I continue to grow,
The jewelry continues to glow,
15 years later, new wax, same mold,
Amazon app click of a button,
Add it to the cart, my book is sold,
That symbol, the threshold that upholds,
This dream never gets old,
I'm being who I was meant to be
I Magnify Faith

Significance

It took Dedication,
To create separation from the life I knew,
To stay more focus on YOU,
And YOU saw me through the blueprint,
through the master plans,
You're the Mastermind,
You already knew that I grow,
I'm humble, there is no show,
the seed is starting to glow,

As I wake up out of my dreams,
I put my right hand to God,
Let me accomplish these wishes,
Let me fulfill these visions,
Let me conquer these goals,
Let me live healthy and bold,
Let me conquer greatness
as it starts to unfold,
Let me remain humble,
Time to move on
from writing books to be sold,
Let them open these books
to see what was I told,
let them understand this gold
"Savior and Stars",
The signature explaining my thoughts
To the all Mighty God,
As I put my right hand to Jesus,
Guide my heart to give more,
Guide me to open the door,
Guide me to what was written,

Significance continued...

Let me accomplish what was mentioned,
Let me be a fisher of men,
Help me Holy Spirit control my sin,
Let me conquer what is within
The desires of this world; money, power and pride,
Holy Spirit please continue to guide,
Let me continue to use this pen,
Let me continue to sign off on things that matter,
Let me understand service is required to
The Master,
The King of Kings,
the Lord of Lords,
Let me continue to give
my time, treasure & talents,
Please create the perfect balance,
I pray to God to put this all into action....
Matthew 6:33

NH

Sovereign

Sailboat

Service is my goal,
To give from my heart,
I double up and pay it forward,
A beautiful piece of art
I'm sharing with the world,
I am small piece of the puzzle,
An ordinary bubble inside of a bottle of bubbles
look at me multiplying,
Grand Cru, a champagne celebration spreading a
little cheer across the timeline,
as I bypass selfishness with sacrifice,
my signature, a small representation of Christ,
the renewal, which is inside of me,
as I set my course like *The Giving Tree,*
let's ride the waves & reflect on how the
wind continues to pull me through,
all along I kind of knew it was YOU
who allowed the breeze to set my path,
a new dream, a new task…
Life moves pretty fast,
no need to wonder, no need to ask,
I am here at last, pen in my hand,
this is just the draft…
The present is my gift,
now let me work on my manuscript 1,2,3,4,5,6…

Sailboat continued...

7 this is it, time for a shift, as I heel,
the equilibrium comes to the right place,
now that I have healed from the past,
as I'm on the path of life,
sometimes I'm entering the unknown
but let it be known,
I have grown, the waves look so familiar,
some I battled as a child,
this time I'm here to deliver more light
to guide others through,
see you got more than you asked for
when you asked about the lapel pin,
the sailboat,
a fisher of men,
Do you know HIM?

Surrender

Goodbye editing,
Goodbye cover creator
Goodbye approval
Hello sand,
Hello water,
Hello you
Call me the breeze
Call me easy as can be
Call me the green light I have to go
Keep me where the light is
Keep me where the love is pure
Keep me where I can be true
I trust that it is time for something new
I trust myself that this is what I want to do
This is what my heart desires
The Signature tagline
Create Enhance Inspire
Smile, no need to publish
"Writing a Dream",
The Signature is my dream,
I converted all files to my Foundation,
I showed how this all began
With the The Mind, the Pen, the paper:
Reflections of the Soul,
I remember writing in my journal 2006,
If I had one wish
It would be to complete the seven books,
At the time I only saw myself,
Then I took the next step & got married,
I said let me do "Discovering Devotion",

Surrender continued...

That's ten years' worth of work,
I can be done with my books
Then a year later, it was a different look,
I'm inspired by the birth of my child,
The fire inside is spreading wild,
The blaze from the dove,
My concentration was still love
But a love from beyond,
I became more confident in my approach,
Now I understood hope,
Even though I thought I knew it before,
New heights caused me to soar,
I'm separating from this notion of
I have to prove this or that,
Give me my dad shoes,
Where is my dad hat?
See my vibe,
Oct 22 he is alive,
He's right here with the others in my heart,
I'm living my dream,
I'm hitting the mark,
Sometimes the great ones are lost,
like the tapes of Nas,
It's time for this Virgo to part,
This a beautiful entry to a brand-new start
It's time to separate some things so,
I can enjoy...

Surrender continued...

If I'm missed on this level,
People have 40, 55, 50,
140, 41, 87 and 7 entries
To read again,
Or maybe read for the first time
It's time for separation
I have crossed the line, it's time to unwind,
The umbrella is in the sand
"Forever and a day" and everything is fine,
Just the three of us,
Just like the beginning,
They were apart me I just didn't know it
But HE did,
Now I'm fully connected
I surrender
Knowing that I'm a child of the King,
praise songs I sing,
JESUS IS LOVE ,
I need you *MORE THAN ANYTHING*,
it's *FOR YOUR GLORY*,
I LOOK TO YOU
because I know *THERE IS MORE*,
when that time comes
IM GONNA BE READY,
GOD IS BLESSING
and *GOD FAVORED ME*,
OH HOW PRECIOUS
I can't believe my *WORTH*,
It was God doing *A GREAT WORK* in me,
ITS WORKING, WONT HE DO IT,
WE'RE BLESSED,

Surrender continued...

FOR THE REST OF MY LIFE
I BELIEVE you are all I need,
there is *NO OTHER NAME* that desires
EVERY PRAISE,
Continue to *SPEAK TO MY HEART,*
I SHALL WEAR A CROWN
because of *THE BEAUTY OF THE CROSS,*
I can *FLY LIKE A BIRD*
because *MY NAME IS VICTORY,*
THANK YOU for *TOMORROW*
It's *SOMETHING ABOUT THE NAME JESUS,*
that gives me peace knowing
I'm *GOING UP YONDER* to heaven
But until that time comes
I will use faith knowing
You used sight beyond what I can see
You know what's in store for me
I am blessed beyond measure
This is what I treasure
Give me the strength to reach the goal
I praise the message for my soul…
Faith, Hope and Charity

Love conquers all

HOSANNA

Forever and Ever and Ever

See page 145

6
Foundation
12

2019

MAJESTIC FORTE
MARCUS YATES FORD

FOUNDATION

Cover Concept by Marcus Yates Ford
Photo & Design by April Reed Mooney
U4U Photography and Graphics

Abundant Beauty from the Cross

I am wishing I could paint the cross on a canvas,
So I must paint the picture with these words
It takes time to analyze each sentence, each line
The reality is when I wear a cross on a necklace
My mind is focused in a new direction
People say that's a nice cross
You mean the diamonds I bought?
Are we not focused on the war HE fought,
So we can have the chance for eternal life?
The wooden cross carried down that road,
Harsh critics from the crowd,
Thrones from the crown
Now my diamonds gleam and sparkle
But the truth is the shine came through
Because darkness could not defeat the light
The coal trying to contain what is meant to be free
Now you can see the beauty of the cross
When the beautiful stone is released
The stone is removed from the tomb
And it shines so bright
When I wear the cross
I know the true beauty of it
It's called sacrifice

No greater love than a friend
That would lay down his life
Foundation 2019

Deeper than what you see

The diamond cross pendant
The meaning more than you can see,
It's not about the why it gleams,
It's about the river streams
Through the lake of my dreams,
The baptism to make me clean,
Asking for forgiveness, repenting of my ways
That separate me from my calling,
That gentle reminder
That the light is always shining,
The Cross
Jesus protected me when I was lost,
The sacrifice that is a priceless cost,
The invitation to a better place,
Heaven my safe haven,
A mansion waiting on streets of gold,
But right now those stones sitting in gold,
I shall wear a crown when it's all over,
My savior has appointed me,
So no matter the struggle or obstacles,
I must remember the true meaning
Of the beauty of the cross,
How You love me so and never let me go,
When life was upside down,
YOU turned it all around,
Yes Jesus Loves me, the beauty of the cross
The symbolism of the Love for others...
Love someone today
Foundation 2019

Enhancement

You enhance my life,
From the moment you were in my arms,
I knew I wanted to be everything
a father is supposed to be,
God guide me to be who I need to be,
And like the giving tree,
I want to share great things with you,
I want to give you everything in this world
to make you happy,
I want to teach you only joy comes from God,
This is critical for our foundation
As humans will disappoint you,
I pray I never disappoint you
And if I do I ask for you to forgive me
And continue to love me for
How God intended me to be,
Your smile and your laugh as pushed me
Through days you can't imagine,
I get sad I think how you will never
Know my brother, your uncle,
It's little things we want to control,
I pray to be there for you,
For each prized moment, that you cherish,
Just the other day you grab my finger
So I could walk with you,
You may think I'm guiding you
But in reality you are guiding me,
You are helping me to keep a clean heart,
To focus on the light and not the dark,

Enhancement continued...

Also to give you all of my kisses
And to focus on all of my wishes,
Which is to love like my Savior...
Sacrifice so you can have the better life...
I love you more than you can imagine.
Foundation 2019

God made me

God made me
Mo City raised me
Houston amazed me
Jesus saved me

If life is a movie
Then the Afterlife is the sequel
Job well done,
the golden gates are open for you,
A mansion set aside
because you were true,
True to your heart
Mama's teachings brought my passion
She was the one
that brought these books to action,
My dad's desire was to get a car with a horse,
So when I needed a new car
I looked at the symbol on the Porsche
Lights, camera, every person is a star
Build a foundation this is how you get this far
Really it's God's Grace, he shows the picture,
I grabbed the pencil and begin to trace,
Sometimes I colored outside the lines,
I'm human I'm not divine,
He said keep coloring everything is fine,
You have freedom of choice
Even though you are my design,
And in due time I came back to HIS intentions,
Look at His artwork
Foundation 2019

Love is Easy

I want to love easy,
I want to erase the pain in my heart,
I want to love like God, the love that's easy,
Only forgiveness
and opportunities for improvement,
I don't want to make it hard,
I want love easy but I keep looking at my scar,
So I look to God
and Jesus shows me HIS' scars,
So I know Love is easy, see where I been,
That's how I made it this far, in the darkness,
HE appeared "the shining star",
So I ask that I love easy,
I ask You to erase all of my doubts,
eliminate my judgements
like I have been better than my counterparts
Because You know I was the one making it hard.
Lord, cleanse my heart,
Let me love easy like You,
Today is my new start
Let me love unconditional
Agape
Foundation 2019

Strings in my Heart

You fixed the strings in my heart,
Your mother was the start
You took the rest and completed the light
When I was in the dark, You're my shining star,
Here and far, you have no idea,
How you erased the pain in my heart,
You have erased the pain
Of me missing your uncle by far,
You will never know him
But you have to understand
He loved me from my start
On days you look at the frames
With the babies playing their part,
The Lord knew you was the part,
To help heal my heart because when I'm with you,
I know how I got this far…love,
Which is the answer from the start
His Grace and mercy,
What is complicated and hard is so easy,
So continue, to smile
And erase your Daddy's pain through the seasons,
Christ is the reason,
Help me as I have committed treason
Of being uneasy of the loss,
You will never know,
But God allowed you to fix the strings in my heart,
your love is easy
And you have helped ease me from the start,
9/6/17 to now,
Love you always, the strings in my heart
Foundation 2019

The Spirit of Sam/Sam Made me Smile

As I sat there and I listened to the stories
I tried to focus only on the glory
Each word little by little
Brought me to a different place
It has been a while since I saw the young boy
Where I remembered his face
He was such a vibrant and cool kid with that charm
As I move along, he was 29 and now he is gone
My mind is in a different space
But I'm in a familiar place
A place where my neighbors love me
As they loved themselves
I received so much love
Those Daily Breads was placed in my hands
Those prayers in the car before school on demand
The Williams family
I would not have made it without you
The sacrifice and the care
As I looked at the program, I stared
I heard the how come and the what if
I listened to the poem to his father and mother,
What a gift, it brings tears to my eyes,
I listened to Isaiah say no one truly dies
The spirit of Sam is alive, He lives in our hearts
Isaiah 57:1, protection from what was to come
I look back at the pictures for a while;
I see the style, I time traveled, I covered miles,
You brought me back to the days with Granny
Sam, you made me smile
Foundation 2019

Fallback

As I fallback to putting pen to paper,
Early in the morning,
What should be the topic to savor?
As I reflect, my struggle is the sip and savor,
Time for a detox, a cleanse of my life,
I have thought about it once
I have thought about it twice,
As I try to channel my introvert-ness,
I continue to get emails
that make me a socialite,
I must be out to sale these books,
So people see who I am
Like Prince "You got the look",
I rather sit at home and cook,
I enjoy these 5am times in my journal,
Quiet time to express my thoughts,
Time change fallback its extra dark,
Detox, paper to pen again is a good start,
A small flame of thoughts ready to spark,
One of my goals is to express this art,
Fallback a renaissance man,
Sunday tunes will be Jazz,
I'll put on the brown robe to be like my dad,
I love you more today than yesterday
But not as much as tomorrow that's Happy Talk,
Fallback one hour back,
Pen to paper, you are back, so I smile
Foundation 2019

Looking Back on Vanity

I'm in love with the better half of me,
The rich black lustrous goatee with the smooth skin
The charm, the hustle to make things happen
What happen, sacrifices made
Some called it maturity, some called it change
I'm losing my ability to see those days
Those personal accomplishments
Mostly faded pictures showing my ego
The younger me, being tested by faith
That drive that made me marketable,
That goal of more gold more money to fold
Life of the young and restless, Life of the Bold
…and the Beautiful
The days were I felt I was the chosen one
Embracing the gift and the curse,
Everybody wants to be a star
Days of our lives, One Life to Live
Trying to build a Dynasty
The other half of me said look at the Guiding Light
Another world and as the world turns
Now I focus on Matthew 6:33 instead of vanity
Foundation 2019

Winter Breeze

California Dreaming is how
I discovered Zion Riots Wear, Venice Beach,
It's something about LA, never thought
Bob Marley shirts would get me paid,
Now I'm relaxing Otis Redding,
Sitting at the dock of the bay,
Time to walk on by like Issac Hayes,
When I received that first payment
It was Happy Feelings
Like Frankie Beverly and Maze,
I'm amazed even today that I saw the wave
As I looked at the waves,
As the time moves away I decided to change lanes,
premium goods shoe wear,
Couriering exclusives in advance,
I took that chance,
That's how I won the contest in the 2nd grade
When I decided to dance,
I went with "that" feeling this may work,
Like Bobby Womack said it's a winter's day
So I stopped into church,
A reflection in my heart, the temple is there
reminding me of my start,
Got on my knees and begin to pray...
5:45 a.m. the alarm goes off Aretha Franklin
Featuring Mavis Staples "O Happy Day",
Quick notes and I'm on my way...
California Dreaming
Foundation 2019

Spiritual Message On My Wrist

Simple creation of expression
Set through my foundation
Revealed to enhance my lifestyle,
Which I hope to inspire others to be
Who they are,
The 14 karat gold is to separate its uniqueness
From what others might try to duplicate,
Really, my skin is sensitive to other metals,
The first piece is sand dollar,
Which represents to teach faith as the five holes
represent the wounds Christ endured.
The center blooms the Easter Lily
With the star of Bethlehem,
The next piece is the dove
To show there is always hope
Of all that believe in Him,
Call his name and safety will overtake you,
When I was stranded in the sea,
His presence was there,
The next piece is the cross,
Reminds me of the sacrifice of Jesus
And for me to sacrifice for others,
The last piece the guardian angel,
I know God has placed one or some in my life,
The overall message of the bracelet is simple,
I'm a child of God
Foundation 2019

Zenith

Something about blue,
It is my foundation as I learn more about You,
The creator of the stars,
I look far in the distance,
My thoughts tell me it's a Virgo thing,
The hues of blue,
The sapphire that explains I'm the earth
You are my birth,
You separated the darkness from the light,
As I reflect on when my life is dark
The light is winning with one spectacle of a twinkle
As I see through a wrinkle in time,
Its time after time the light prevails,
Something about blue has a story to tell,
It's simple, be calm the light will appear
Foundation 2019

5
Inspirations
8

2018

Inspirations

Majestic Forte
MARCUS YATES FORD

Cover Concept by Marcus Yates Ford
Photo & Design by April Reed Mooney
U4U Photography and Graphics

The Prelude: The Pulpit

I'm a poetic writer not a poetic reciter,
I'm not here to entertain the crowd
This is my therapy, which keeps me on the ground
The reward I seek
Is when YOU speak my name in the Book of Life
I know I have done plenty of wrong
However, my heart wants to do plenty of right
I repent of my sins
I will use Freedom of the Mind; the open mic,
To spread Your Word and shed Your light
I will speak the truth; I can't make it without YOU
Give me the strength; be by my side
As I deliver the words that I wrote down
Let them reach like the Sermon on the Mount
It's about the mind, the pen, and the paper
That will show the reflections of my soul
It's time to be bold,
My legacy is to live in the streets of gold
Therefore, I will use Love, Grace and Imani
As part of the journey to Discover Devotion
It was YOU that saved me from the ocean;
More accurately the Caribbean Sea
Through Your teachings, it brought me peace
Speak to my heart so I can be the best version of me
Let me accomplish my goals
Directed by YOU piece by piece
Inspirations from God, the 5th book We released

Colossians 3:23
Inspirations 2018

Victory

When you first opened up your eyes,
I said they look so familiar
Like I have been looking at them for a lifetime.
My baby girl, I am mesmerized
As I stare like what a wonder...
Tears flow inside of me
And I pray for a lifetime with you...
God's WORD is so true,
So I must dedicate you back to HIM,
I have to trust HIM with you...
HE brought me this far,
What a miracle to see, a Victory, for us,
I pray that you only have the best from us,
You are our miracle,
All the things we never knew,
You are our miracle look at what GOD can do,
HE made us a perfect you,
We pray for you to accomplish
All of your dreams and to enjoy the world
We brought you into,
And with joyful cares and humble hearts,
We will always love you

Jeremiah 1:5   Psalms 127:3

Inspirations 2018

Name Above All Names

I will have the courage
To proclaim the name above all of names
There is No other name
That can heal me
There is No other name
That can give me vision
There is No other name
That can give me joy
There is No other name
That can give me wisdom
There is No other name
That can bring me out of darkness
There is No other name
That can put me on the path of righteousness
There is No other name
That can forgive me
There is No other name
That can take me higher
There is No other name
That can give me the truth and light
There is No other name
That can show me what is right
There is No other name
That is there when I call
There is No other name
That is there when I fall
There is No other name
That speaks to my heart

Name Above All Names continued

There is No other name
That can put me together when I'm apart
There is No other name
That is light as a feather
There is No other name
That can change the weather
There is No other name
That can make me better
There is No other name
That can quench my thirst
I will have courage to put the Messiah first
There is only one name "Jesus"

Philippians 2:9
Inspirations 2018

This is your Life

As I reflect on where I have been or better yet
where YOU have taken me
I am still amazed at how much YOU Love me
The path of destruction I embraced
The scars that show the trace of the mistakes
But the stories I'm able to tell
Because YOU brought me through...
When I was alone it was only YOU,
YOU lifted me,
YOU took care of me,
YOU helped me escape,
YOU saved me,
YOU healed me,
YOU comforted me...
Now I can only attempt to show my gratitude
By speaking Your name, Explaining to others how
YOU brought me through the storms....
The sunshine is a testimony of the victory,
LORD thank YOU
For the new blessings YOU have put in my life,
I never dreamed of this life,
That I'm somebody's husband and father,
That I'm the spiritual leader for
My child and my wife...
Your WILL has brought me through
And this is just the beginning

2 Timothy 1:8-12
Inspirations 2018

I Choose

I choose to love
Because it heals
I choose to focus on the present
Because I cannot change the past
I choose to forgive
Because it is the only way for me to live
I choose to have hope
Because it carries me to places of purity
I choose to express joy
Because it is inside me,
Given to me by the GodHead
I choose to be thankful
Because I realize things could be worse
I choose to be humble
Because I see I am here by grace
I choose to help
Because I am in touch with sympathy and empathy
I choose to listen
Because it is what completes me
I choose to travel light
With the essentials of love, hope and faith
Because that is all I need at any destination
Or in any situation
Inspirations 2018

The Lamp

If this is called Poetry
Then I have been writing ever since '81,
When I picked up Silverstein,
A Light in the Attic
I have been writing since I was five,
Now that is mathematic,
Very enlightened, go purchase
A Light in the Attic
Because it's a light in this attic
That shines bright
Enough to generate electricity
Touch this man and feel this static
My knowledge is shocking like thunder
It is lighting when I start to wonder
Brainstorming is upon us,
December of '75
They would lie to create a gift,
9/10/76
I would arrive,
Better known as the prince
The scion, Your majesty,
Majestic Forte the blueprint
The scroll,
A connection to the KEY
Give me the courage
To be who YOU called me to be
A disciple of Christ…
Matthew 5:14-16
Inspirations 2018

May Peace be with you

If the good die young
And we get better with age
The best potential has been buried
But their soul has been saved

A tombstone message at their grave
Alternative version
Let their ashes be scattered among the waves

I see the pain in their face;
Their tears flow with ease
I pray you didn't
Absorb their pain in their transition
I pray you were at peace
And listening to the Angels' whispers
Joy for the Journey, time for the next adventure

As long as I breathe, you breathe
As long as I laugh, you laugh
As long as I smile, you smile
Lives you have touched,
Those will be the thoughts
among them and us:

Rest in peace for all the ones we have lost
Wear your crown
Inspirations 2018

A Connoisseur's Limited Release

Are you ready?
Because I'm ready for *Ready* to open,
Sometimes you just want to go where
Everybody knows your name
We are just ordinary people;
We are all the same, Sinners saved by Grace
I am at my new favorite place
Let us order a bottle of champagne,
Let us celebrate life
Pop, fizz, clink
I like to enjoy a Rose'
With the color of an immaculate pink
This is what I call a refreshing drink
Let us put that bottle on ice
As I reflect about me life,
I celebrate the Victory
How God made a way,
How he brought me through night
There is joy in the morning,
No more darkness only the Light
My foundation is intact;
Faith has brought me through the storms
Love has brought me through the attacks
Hope has always pushed me ahead
So many tears through the years
Trials and Tribulations James 1:3
I am thankful for this toast
"Cheers"
Inspirations 2018

4
Discovering Devotion
24

2016

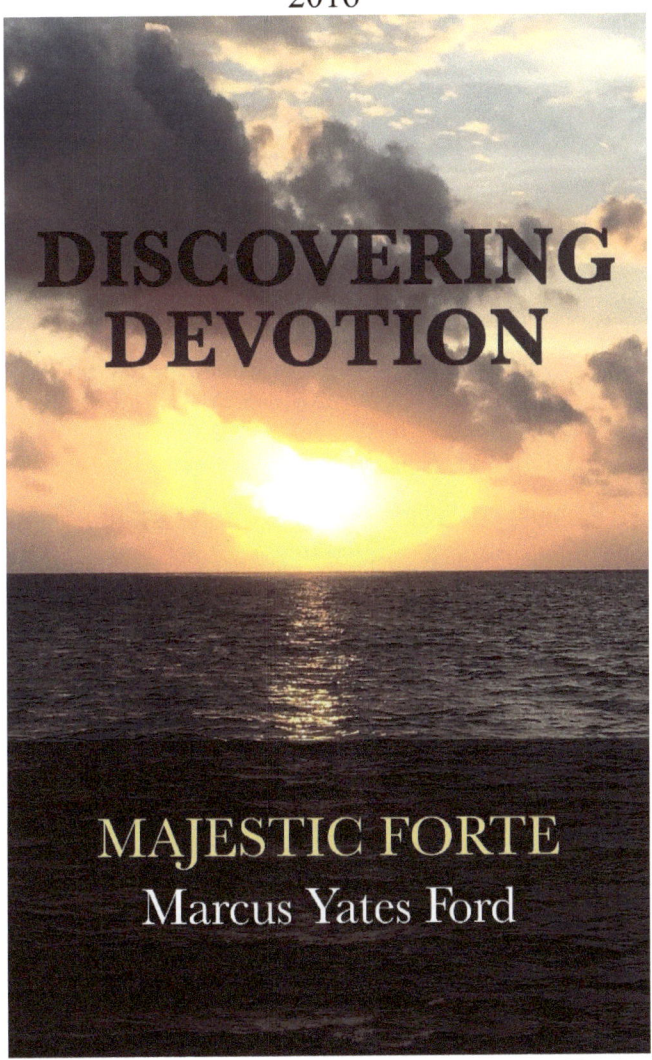

Cover Concept & Design by Marcus Yates Ford

All Eyes on You

(I tried to wait because)
I wanted to tell you face to face
But I was forced to use my force of writing
The strokes, Encrusted in my fingers
Are the pen to these pages
So many thoughts, so many feelings,
So many words, *You must read these pages*
Like a bird trapped in a cage
I must release, so I can glide to freedom
I want to go to the end of the earth
To watch the sunset on a perfect evening
Or
Watch my watch on the night, the morning
will make a new season
Patience, I'm achieving
You are the reason; I love with ease
Years ago you planted seeds
and now they have grown
I have learned to love you more at a distance
than in the present
My future is new, I grew, the life I drew
I'm in eternity looking back
I flew, I fly, and I grow
I draw; this is the life I saw, this is what I see
Years have passed; my eyes were all on you
Now, I am in the mirror and all eyes are on You
Look what I have been through;
all I can do is smile
Because I want to tell you, I want to show You
Now I see the Christ in you
Discovering Devotion 2016

In My Heart
(Inspired by the movie "In my Country")

When I do rewind time,
I'm in a powder blue Benz
Cooling out to the sound of jazz,
Enjoying the passenger's ride,
The ole man shifting gears
The car he steers,
He guides,
Those moments taught me: my drive.
We are an image of God,
So that would make you
the greatest man alive,
Short of glory but saved by grace,
I use my pencil and erase your mistakes,
My fingerprints; the lines you trace.
I'm doing this from my journal
but one day I will do it face to face,
Accomplishing the term and the meaning...
To **Embrace.**

Thank you, Pops for those rides to church and you picking me up from school.
Discovering Devotion 2016

Boarding Pass Please

My soul is driven;
I'm solely driven by the Spirit; the ambition
My vision by the prism, the colors of the ray,
The opportunities that come my way
The ability to communicate
through this pen, once again
I'm boarding a plane; the higher I aim,
the harder it is to fall
Because it's a long way down,
so I settle for who I am now
So I open and read my journal, my own book
What did it take?
The advice from others,
I learned from their mistakes
Faith, I embraced
I'm headed to a new destination,
A long runway, so I must be patient
A new administration, same dictation
My freedom,
my feel good is created through these works
The scion is birthed with the gift and the curse
Worldly pleasures but a product of the church
My temple, my journal,
My explanation of Karma
I never took time to wonder or to research
I just step out of the box
I released "Freedom of the Mind"
To show I was hot

Boarding Pass Please continued

I'm the blueprint, I'm the poet in the art;
reference John Holyfield
I create art that creates a spark
I express what's in my heart like paint brushes
I use strokes to hit the mark,
My pen, when it hits the paper;
A new message begins
A new journey, a new topic, as we descend
Secure your tray tables, seats in their upright
positions and fasten your seat belts
We are close to my vision
The wheels come down;
These are words from your captain above
Welcome to your final destination, the state of ……
Discovering Devotion 2016

Savior & Stars

Expression through art,
Which is words, symbols, metals and stones
I give a message through charms
And a gold necklace
Let me explain
My perspective of my new treasure
My sign pure like a virgin
My birth month is a blue sapphire;
Which is so meek
Gold coin immersed through the fire
Numbers engraved
To show the numbers from astrology
However, the numbers have a biblical meaning
Just like Georgetown's Answer is a 3
In my life it's the Trinity
The perfect 3
God, Jesus, and the Holy Spirit
Then, the number 5 I focus on the Law
The first five books of the Bible; The Law
So I focus on the five commandments
with God
And the five commandments with others
Next, the number 6,
to remind me of being a man
Our fatal flaw within;
We lean on our own understanding
This is our human weakness,
So I remember we are nothing without God
That is why I need 12, the perfect number

Savior & Stars Continued

My Lord is the only one
With all the power and authority
Then the number 20, the perfect waiting period
Lord guide me in the direction
you want me to go
Show me what you want me to know
So I use 27, the New Testament,
Which is all its books
This is vital for my growth, quench my thirst
The Virgo, the element; I must water my earth
The other charm so simple,
Yet so complicated; The Cross
You represent the church,
My Lord and Savior on Cavalry
Sacrifice for a wretch like you and me
The charm necklace around my neck
Represents more than
what the naked eye can see
Some only like the way it twinkles and glistens
Discovering Devotion 2016

The Wishing Well

I knew I dreamed of this life before
I created this moment of the pen
Touching the paper
Lessons, my parents taught me
About values and principles
Spiritual connection, virtues and blessings
To my adulthood
Serving a purpose of the inner beauty
Deleting superficial appearances
The truth of the Bible's pages
Gave me endurance
I confessed which gave me assurance
That my dream is reality
The streets of gold
I have mapped on my navigation system
My ambition creates the facts of my sentence.
The formula is to listen to the spirit
The wings that flap
Do you hear it?
My angels make their appearance
And give me clearance.
This dream, when I flip that *coin* into the well
This is what I was wishing.
Discovering Devotion 2016

The Crowd of My Thoughts

As I step back
and look at the crowd of my thoughts
A brief reunion of my memories occurs
The renewal of the past my mind brings
But I don't ask questions
I sit back and enjoy the answers
The mile markers as stepping-stones,
the blueprint of my achievements
I embrace what got me here;
my instincts, my dreams,
And my planning
I'm happy where I am, as I move forward
I travel light with an open mind
No need for preconceptions,
stereotypes or being biased
I'm at Niagara Falls, beautiful scene,
Multi cultures enjoying nature's finest
No war, no arguments, no eyes of mistrust
Only body language saying
"Can you snap a picture of us"
As the water falls at the waterfalls,
The crowd of my thoughts tells it all

This is unbelievable
Discovering Devotion 2016

Volume II of my Life

The affection of serenity and desire,
I'm going higher, beyond my thoughts,
Lessons learned, I have been taught,
Music eases my soul, guides my mind
I'm relaxed, sun shines in, blue skies,
White clouds, my red heart, a better day,
I'm moving along my way,
What more can I say but everything is okay,
Slowly I heal; I still pray for my peers,
My nightmares still bring fears,
As I look in the mirror, new haircut,
New beard, a little salt and pepper,
Takes some time
But I'm getting used to this look,
They say its aging with grace, I laugh but
I guess that's what puts the smile on my face,
I'm ready for a new take…take 1…
I'm having fun being me and as far as I can see,
No more need for facades, no masks,
No putting up fronts, this is who I am,
If they can't accept me for whom I am,
Then sorry, we don't have to coexist,
All I have is love in my heart
And heaven on my mind,
With that combined,
Everything else is a flat line,
The beauty of this dream is coming true,
The way it flows, blessings, start to pour,

Volume II of my Life continued

Lord knows, the way you make me enjoy this
position, I love this extension,
The way you made me a better man…
Your humble servant, resident of dreamland…
The way you complete me, the way you…
Discovering Devotion 2016

The MF Signature

Remember on your darkest nights
You are like the onyx stone
If you get close enough you will see the light,
Which will bring you peace
It will keep you in touch with your spirituality
And ultimately give you tranquility
Just like the sweet sounds
That the breeze makes in a seashell
As the thoughts come together,
And I come down from high altitude
I stare beyond the water
I reassess my goals and my dreams
What might seem a little less
Than what I strive to become or even better?
Better yet, I have realized through time,
Something so simple
That it is greater than any material good or reward,
It is the Acknowledgement of Love,
Which brings peace
Only putting my signature on things
That glorify God
Go Jesus Go
Discovering Devotion 2016

Love Me (Prelude to Love)

You can't love too much one part of me
You should not love only one part of me
You shouldn't love only the way the words read
You should love every part of me
Discovering Devotion 2016

Dangerous
(My Imagination)

You're dangerous, I can't control myself,
and I can't stop touching you
You're dangerous as I lay next to you,
I can't get enough of you
You're dangerous as I start kissing you,
It's over and over my lips on yours;
I draw back and say, "You're so dangerous"
As I continue, I don't have a clue;
You say it's all about me,
No baby it's all about you
You say it's all about me, now that may be true
Because the way you look at me,
The way you use your words,
The way you kiss my lips,
The way you do those things,
They way you use those verbs,
You bring such action,
The way you and I create magic,
No way to contain it, you're so dangerous,
The perfect imperfect stranger,
That has my thoughts thinking of
The moments of being next to you
In that perfect angle, kissing your lips so slow,
Just lying next to you;
I know that you are dangerous
All it took was one kiss
And now I can't stop thinking about you

Dangerous continued

You're so dangerous, the things I do,
The writings about you
You're so dangerous
O yes its true
What I'm I to do?
In my dreams I find myself falling for you
All along I knew that you were dangerous
But my curiosity attracted me to you,
Look at the canvas look at what I drew,
The painting of me all over you
You're dangerous
But I knew it wouldn't stop me
From holding you,
Holding you so close that you knew
That I was dangerous too

My imagination of a you
Discovering Devotion 2016

Cycle

Wait a minute…for the
Fourth time since tears ago,
Three years of a hiatus,
Two versions,
One result
…My dream is here
My true colors I express to you with
Yellow spiders, yellow tulips, yellow flowers,
Our desire of friendship I keep close,
Red hearts, red gold, red roses,
Rose' Champagne,
Let's toast!!!
My brown eyes, my brown skin,
The brown tree trunk,
The inside shows the layers of growth,
Do you see how I have grown?
My black hair, my black pride,
My black diamonds still shine,
In a matter of time,
My book will guide you right to my heart
And you will see I thank the heavens above
For white doves, the white sparks,
My light in the dark
The yellow necklace I wear
Reminds me of my teachings
The inscription on the tag reads
Matthew 22: 37-40
Discovering Devotion 2016

Forever & a Day

As the seasons come and go,
The leaves prepare to change colors
I think about you, "Forever & a Day"
As the sun shines through,
What a sun rise at daybreak
Lying next to you,
I wouldn't want it any other way
The purple skies emerge as you I hold so close;
We are sharing the experience of your view
As I prepare myself with love with limits,
Psychological boundaries
And mental force fields
The hot showers
Bring the essence of this question
Are you the one for "Forever & a Day"?
As I go through the day I contemplate;
Forever is a mighty long time away
But with the breeze, the way the wind blows;
It buries those thoughts deep in my mind
As I enjoy the ocean, the Pacific to be specific
The order of chaos is no where to be found
It's a clear vision of boats and humble transitions
As the lights hit off an object creating a prism,
The waves speak as I sit back and listen;
They remind me of my mission
This is to display my simple human nature;
To give and help those in need
As I walk along the beach,
I stop and insert the umbrella in the sand
I stand and look deep within…
Discovering Devotion 2016

Stars and Entrapment

The stars, my vision as I lay on the rooftop,
The stars call my name, what a beautiful sight,
Pitch-black sky with silver lights,
Five edges so bright,
If you were a woman, I could kiss you forever,
…Until you fade away
And when I thought I lost you,
You would appear another day;
You shine and make each moment magical,
So you are more of everlasting...
Astronomy would say your discovery is fantastic,
As I establish the order of a word of such
immaculate proportion,
A beautiful emotion,
I lay here under the stars and understand that
"silence is golden"
Discovering Devotion 2016

Revamp

I don't think I want to love you anymore
I think I want to stand clear of you
I know I can't survive in your atmosphere
I don't think I want to call you anymore dear
I think I want to stand clear of you
I can't control my heart when I'm around you
Please gravity; keep me down to earth
Luv, you took me so high,
My thoughts are on orbit in another space
In my dreams we always embrace
But my reality has replaced
that moment with silence from one another
Even though it's for a brief moment
I don't think I want to hear from you anymore
I rather keep my memories in my heart
I'm going to stand clear of you
…Because
I think I fall in love again
If, I was in your presence

Booking my flight Home
And now everything is perfect again
Discovering Devotion 2016

Tranquility

Take me to another zone
"Where you are not alone",
There is no "Hole in my soul,
"And "My mind is my home"
As I embrace the wind,
The words come with such ease
Laughing out loud,
Did "Someone move my Cheese?"
Really I don't care,
As I sit here looking
At the nature of the present
Palm trees, specular weather
As I take a deep breath, I get it all together
Magical thoughts "wherever there is good,
It can only get better"
Immaculate structure of words being delivered
...from my thoughts
Intoxicating view brings a "new" translation:
True words from the heart
One small spark can create a great flame;
A great flame was created by a little spark
My thoughts still remain extraordinary,
"extra" ordinary,
Even through delightful frustrations
The world moving at my speed, perfect rotation
As I search the globe for world destinations,
"Where else should I go?"
As my mind departs from dreamland,

Tranquility continued

My pride is intact with my IPOD
In the cargo pocket of my khaki pants
Or what would you say the difference is
If I called them tan?
I am in tune, just my imagination,
As I consume, Peaceful thoughts on Earth
Waiting on a vacation
Discovering Devotion 2016

Bonfire

From the blaze, the heat, the sparks
The light in the dark
Creating the path straight to the heart
Says let's keep the line full of dance,
Round and round let's twirl under the stars
Watch the sea turtles flap on the sand
We hold hands, as we look at history,
So romantic darling, now she's a Starling,
We are under the Star Light,
Their summer night, there is a sight
Looking at the bride and groom
The rose gold is starting to bloom
What a Joyful June,
From the wonders in Rome,
The finesse of Florence,
The couture of Milan,
Riding in the gondolas in Venice,
The magic of the wedding
On Nicaragua's Emerald Coast,
The Pacific blue we admire

Strike a match…

Watch the fireworks…

Dance

Bonfire
Discovering Devotion 2016

Unselfish

Listen…my love…I let love take control of me
Even though it's not you I see
My unselfishness didn't want you to hurt again
Daily love signals to you I send
I didn't bend every moment I wanted you back
I only thought of the distance of Virginia
So I put my pride to the front instead of the back,
The pain I hold inside
Life with love you can't hold is a prison
I don't reach because I know the reason
My love wants you to be pleased living life at ease
My heart you hold the master keys
I walked away knowing, what else could I do?
Only fault is how much I love you
So I chose not to disappoint you again
My eagerness for you I held within
So I live by the golden rule
That's why I left, no true effort, I flew
Because I know what the real phrase means that…
"I love you"
Discovering Devotion 2016

The Afterthought (Epilogue)

As I have moved on from *A Heart that Cries*
I think of the summer moon & the winter sun
I use my fingers to trace the calendar
And look at the days and years
When you were in my arms
And you rescued me Luv
When I look at the purple skies above,
I smile at those memories realizing that
The heartbreak was worth
The chance of becoming complete.
As I pick up the pieces and move forward
The time that was taken from me has created
My thoughts of a beautiful appreciation
As I smile and laugh,
Now I can leave all bags behind
As I reflect on those
Magical moments and times with you
Love, Grace and now Faith;
Shows me what it takes
To not be scared of heartbreak
And to pursue growth with you
For the rest of my life
I thank God that I finally got it right
I love the way you love me
I'm dedicate to the divine direction of our future
Husband and Wife
Discovering Devotion 2016

My Greatest Work

With the power of the pen, it begins,
the dream that is
I create scene after scene, the milestone I reach
What is knowledge if you don't teach?
Creative marketing, concepts, and ideas I share
I write it so you can get it, this vision
Line for line, sentence by sentence
Time for a revision,
In high school favorites I wasn't mentioned
Most likely to Succeed, Most Witty
Let us revisit, Most Attractive, Best Dressed
In that school system
Who would have thought years later
I would demand attention
My extension is to excel; I'm living well
The exception to those pages
In those hallways I did dwell
Who am I you ask?
Lets be exact they didn't have a category for me
Mr. Nonchalant, Mr. Laidback
Now as I sit back, I'm so relaxed
Not boasting just stating facts, what do I lack?
Mr. All That, the demand not to be famous
Staying modest and humble
Seeking no reward on Earth
I'm focused on my reward in heaven
I'm here because of Grace and Mercy
Thanking you Lord for your blessing
Discovering Devotion 2016

When Everything is Meant to be Broken

When everything is meant to be broken,
I lie down
And wait for the sun to come up the next day
I stay encouraged; let me be a pillar of faith
When everything is meant to be broken,
I pray for mercy and God's Grace
As I transition in this economy's pace
And family affairs,
It can create a bitter taste
Nightmares try to strike and hit their target;
Trying to get me to focus on what is no longer
When everything is meant to be broken,
I only get stronger
I'm at the door of reality
And I'm prepared for the war of the unknown
I'm waiting and accepting the challenge
Of the construction of an image
As I walk to the edge,
My intention is to save myself and be independent;
When it comes to the happiness in my heart,
I will still give, share and help;
Being Christ-Like
I'm trying to conquer
The mentality of leaning on my own understanding
Don't want to be that type
Everything is meant to be broken
That way God can make us whole,
So we know there is no way without Him
Because He is in control

When Everything is Meant to be Broken...

As I breathe through these times
Of doubt and encouragement,
I approach this situation as a mercenary,
With only smiles to gain;
My payment is to touch someone's life
and try to ease the pain
As I promote Peace, Spirituality, and Tranquility
through a bracelet
So if everything is meant to be broken,
I will face forward in humanity,
Knowing life is great.
Discovering Devotion 2016

Higher Calling

My higher calling is to give spiritual messages
through a poetic form
I'm on the next train; I'm going beyond my norm
I'm in the pulpit reaching toward the truth
I will inspire the youth
Adults, do you understand these truths?
Breakdown the dream,
It's not about the green and the means,
It's about elevating, relating, anticipating,
administrating that power,
To teach the youth; the truth, the love,
the message of team,
About how to dream, make goals,
Now, its money we fold,
We walk the skies above, the streets of gold,
Now, that is writing a dream, expressing truth
I was told, I was made of clay; So God could mold
Discovering devotion, Is a book of prayers next?
What is my best?
New method I introduced, I saw the footprints
So I knew what to do, I followed my mind;
I set aside my ways, I have new drives,
Which are poems that are God driven
I'm a visionary completing a vision.
Prayers in Jesus' name, forgive me
I ask for repentance, so I can go back to His image
Let me revisit and absorb, I analyzed this poem
Now you comprehend and listen,
Go back and listen to the sentences
And you will understand what I mentioned
Discovering Devotion 2016

The Creativity I make

I wish for peace, happiness for within,
Help me Lord understand my faults,
and why my world is apart?
Your son is coming to you, my Father
I have been trying harder
To express love and to forgive,
I need your help so I can live
What do I have to give?
I gave my life on that day,
Baptize in that Oklahoma River
July 31, 1987
I was release from prison;
You overturn my sentence
I seem so timid
But through my life that was my best decision
The feeling of being so pure
When I came up from that water
Same image as my Father,
Through time sin push me
Farther away from you
Now, I'm repaying you by being an author
Spreading the truth on how you save
And uplift this slave
To the material world,
Heartache from those women,
Ladies, I strive to be a good man
Giving all that I can, short of glory,
However, saved by grace
Gifted with the writings I make
Teaching love burying hate,

The Creativity I make continued

I patiently wait
Renewing all things, I keep my faith
One day I will dance
With my grandparents by the pearly gates
My goal to touch the world
And put a smile on their face
Lord through my good,
I hope I can erase my mistakes
At least replace,
Thank you Lord for these gifts of grace,
I'm here for you to take and make great
And spread your truth
This is what I owe back to you,
For saving me, that's why I do what I do
Words can't express how I love you
Discovering Devotion 2016

Prayer

How could you love me when I was cursing?
How could you love me
When I refuse to be rebirth?
How could you love me
When I didn't put us first?
How could you love me
When I was cheating on you?
How could you love me
When I lost confidence in me?
How could you love me
When I never told you I miss you?
How could you love me
When I thought it was too late?
How could you love me
When it was an error and not a mistake?
How could you love me
When I refuse to go to your place?
How come you continue to be there
for me in this race?

Thank you for your forgiveness and grace
I love you Jesus
Discovering Devotion 2016

"The After Day"

The day after…
In my mind the voice of your laughter,
Us playing with no ideas of the world beyond
The innocent times of our thoughts
And desires to have fun and to compete,
Whether it was video games
Or racing down the street, or mind games;
Making decisions on a board game…Stratego
"The After Day" brings me pain,
A missing piece in my heart,
As I reflect that you have been
With me from the start.
Sundays will never be the same
As I pat you telling you it's ok, you ran hard.
As I look at your face,
I reflect on how I believe you could do anything,
You had the magic plans,
The way you had charisma to coordinate outfits,
The way you had the heart to fight,
The ability of endurance,
That push a big brother has…
I never thought of "The After Day",
Now I feel empty but complete
I still hear you telling me good job,
You did well, and you completed my wishes,
Thank you for being unselfish…
I live with the fact;
I wanted you for the day after,
However "The After Day" is here
I must cherish the bittersweet
Realizing that you are gone.

"The After Day" continued

The energy left my hand
But I know you are at the white cloud,
Smiling, telling me well done,
Now do even better,
You are right! We will always be together
And the bond as brothers is forever…
I smile now because you rest easy
Discovering Devotion 2016

Pray

If you love this man...
Then pray for this man
If you care for this man...
Then pray for this man
If you like this man...
Then pray for this man
If you admire this man...
Then pray for this man
If you know this man...
Then pray for this man
If you see this man...
Then pray for this man
If you hear this man...
Then pray for this man
....

The best gift I will ever receive is prayer
So pray for me during the seasons, the weather
Help me weather the storms,
Pray that my house is a home
Pray that in my heart, I'm not alone,
Pray for my health,
Pray for me, when I'm gone to another zone
Pray for this man,
That I look good on the first of the month
Pray for my protection, pray for more blessings
Because all of this,
I have already prayed for you
I ask you to pray for whom?
I ask you to pray for me.
Discovering Devotion 2016

3
The Freedom of the Mind: The Open Mic
8

2006

Cover Concept & Design by Edward Thornton III
& Marcus Yates Ford

First Stage (I Recite)

I'm a poetic writer, not a reciter,
On stage entertaining the crowd
Snaps, I hear the sound
This is my therapy (my journal),
Which keeps me on the ground
Keeps me in touch with my soul,
On pace with my goals
I promote faith;
Patiently I wait for peace of mind
Coming in due time, as I live,
I give from the heart
Pushing love to hit its mark
With God's grace, this is how I start
Taking this to the next level
I'm still willing and able
And like Abel I will give you my best fruits
I will speak the truth;
I cannot make it without you
Give me the strength;
Be by my side as I deliver the words
I wrote down
Let them reach like the Sermon on the Mount
Don't let the world break me down,
Or tear me apart, be my light in dark
Let these words hit the mark
Let love be released from the heart
Let this spoken word be a good start

First Stage (I Recite) continued

If I fail, please let me be caught
But I have faith that someone will taught
With your love I will survive
This is the true meaning of getting high
Because in order to succeed, you must first try
Jesus be with me
Freedom of the Mind: Open Mic 2006 (edited)

September 10th

From 9/10,
Started at 10:11am sent from heaven
Friday morning me and Mama together
After New Year's has begun
Each year it is 243 plus 10, you have son
Sometimes it is 254 if it leaps
Most accurate it 37 weeks
From the King Holiday to Valentine's,
To the day of the Irish
To Easter Sunday we admire,
To Mother's day is inspired
Memorial Day for veterans;
R.I.P and to ones who are retired
Then Father's Day to 4th, rockets and fireworks,
To a woman's worth
The 19th, my mother's birth
21 days later a baby boy is on earth
I take advantage of each chance,
I do my September dance,
Like Earth, Wind and Fire,
Thanking Mama for birth of the man
Listen Pops, 9/10 I advanced,
A day before the towers fell
In 2001 (paying homage)
Don't worry it's a new plan

September 10th continued

I am building standing tall,
2016 Discovering Devotion, I gave it my all
25 years later from my days in high school
As a crusader to the ridge, I sealed the bridge
September 10th, I live, thanking God,
It is my birthday again
Freedom of the Mind: Open Mic 2006 (edited)

The Scion

Am I the scion to poetry?
Did Langston Hughes know I would come?
He pointed to the family tree
And said he could be the one
Not like Shakespeare with a heroic tragedy
More like focusing on my Majesty
The way HE gives me the words
The nouns, the verbs; my image he curves
Well-rounded, spiritual essence,
Rock solid presence
I live on the surface,
Knowing the ways of the world
The get around, I cool out to the sound of Jazz
I am here at last, run fast to listen to the words
Of the truth, confessions in a wall less booth
My heartaches, I stay focused on a blessing
Looking for a message, Sleepless nights Seattle
I'm restless but not young; no soap opera
From the bottom to the top I climb
My linkage to the royal family of poetry
The blueprint; I am coming
One by one I pay homage,
The women Giovanni &
Angelou made me grow
Depression I deliver like Edgar Allen Poe
My words continue to flow
Shakur gave me the strength of the youth
David gave me the humanity
To speak about You

The Scion continued

Psalms, I use my palms to tilt the hand
To praise the Lord,
The family tree in the branches,
I am just trying to show I belong
The scion
Freedom of the Mind: Open Mic 2006 (edited)

The Blueprint

Motivation to achieve my goals,
I am the one painted by John Holyfield
In that tree
The poet, that's me
Bobby Womack smooth,
It is *just my imagination*
Delivering words to who is in my company
I have the ability to show pain and depression
Like Edgar Allen Poe,
The blade from the pendulum
That swings back and forth,
That can cut you slow
I am a survivor from the pit
I have the ability to express like Maya Angelou
Revision,
A phenomenon man is in your presence
See my glow!
Can I entertain the crowd like Nikki Giovanni?
That remains to been seen
Her delivery, humorous
But serious about real issues
She could be a painter
The way she paints the scene
Thug Life tatted on her arm
Like the poets before me,
Do you see my charm?
I have a dream, like a train, I release steam
With the passion of Tupac, the open mic,

The Blueprint continued

I recite reparations,
Political troubles, militia mind
America is a great big puzzle
And where do we fit?
With a pen and a paper, I am well equipped
My mind thinking past this mortal body,
this flesh
I just use "you" to express and to release stress
These words and rhymes are more than lines
Forward to rewind,
This is the blueprint to a poet's mind
Majestic Forte…
The new news
Giving thanks,
Phyllis Wheatley,
Langston Hughes
Freedom of the Mind: Open Mic 2006 (edited)

Confusion

With feelings mix like chocolate with chips
How do I separate what is deeply dipped
Like peanut butter it's a hard mix and it sticks
The mind wonders like a hard habit to kick
It's like medicine but I'm not sick
The realization of this motivation intervene
The frustration of dealing with this situation
New path, new task, love in the past
Living life, more questions to ask
No smoke, no liquor in a flask
I mediate to realize the wonders
I walk in the tunnel, where questions are among us
Confusion
How do I take this chips out of this ice cream?
No answers in my dreams
No deleted scenes
No commentary to tell me what this means
Maybe one can separate two to make one
Then maybe again the confusion is done
Or maybe it's just begun

Or maybe it's called being love
Freedom of the Mind: Open Mic 2006 (edited)

Creation

As I enter the lab with a pen and a pad
I work like a scientist, who is mad
Chemicals I combine,
Metaphors and similes that rhyme
Poetic lines, mental gestures,
test tubes that measure
Key ingredients that help me perform
Not thinking like the norm,
ever since I was born
I stood out, first place ribbons all my life
The exception I just did things better
Witty, very clever,
I am on the highway to heaven
To the Source; my Creator
Trying to be more like Him instead of a raider
More of a crusader,
my mission is to use my gift
Simple and plain, the reason why I came
To show love and try to heal
I won't enjoy my success but my family will
They won't understand until I'm gone
And try to study my bones,
They'll realize a poet that is great,
They'll realized I can't be cloned
The X and Y chromosome
They are puzzled like the twilight zone
No comparing me at all
I am on another adventure,

Creation continued

They failed to mention or to listen,
To see the vision
It is clear I am from another dimension
Now that I have your attention
The answer is I'm made in God's image
And so are you
Freedom of the Mind: Open Mic 2006 (edited)

Request

You can either love me or leave me alone
But I won't cry no song; *song cry* plays in the car
The audio moves me along
They never miss you until you are gone
My heart always gave you a home
But it's not what you want
Your only ask is a big task
So maybe you should pass
Or maybe change your priorities
And make me a grab
So I can't understand
So all I ask is for you to pray for this man
Send me a boomerang but not the movie
But a lady that's ready for a commitment
One that is five stars like the Four Seasons
A love like no other, the final reason
It's just us together, delicate like a feather
Lady, I'm on the escalator waiting for the next level
Freedom of the Mind: Open Mic 2006 (edited)

500

Love has no limit
I'm just a Disciple of Christ in this world
I just live in it
Corrupted by diamonds and jewels
Setting aside my rules
I'm listening to B.B. King trying to catch the blues
But I have no reason to be blue, I just got the news
Another 500 books sold
That's 500 souls I reach
That's an opportunity
For 500 people for God to teach
As I recite prayer poems as if I preach
The reality of it, I wrote them for what I seek
Praying for my life, for my soul to keep
I'm in front of the church,
Real tears of joy, I weep
Discovering Devotion coming soon!
Freedom of the Mind: Open Mic 2006

2
Love, Grace and Imani
10

2005

Cover Concept & Design by Marcus Yates Ford

Who am I?

Who am I, the youngest son from Ms. Ford
Who am I, the son of the mighty Lord
As I walked through the valleys
Not knowing what's in store
Are we living to die? Is that what we are here for?
Who am I, the man here to express thoughts & love
Who am I, the son sent from the heavens above
As I look at my chain and pendant, I see Jesus
He is the reason I stand and I'm breathing
Who am I, the man that stands for
Forgiveness of the soul
The one that makes the ice cube cold
Who I am, a man that borrows this body to teach
The one that breaks bread and says let us eat
The one that will wipe tears from those who weep
Drink this blood and it is I you seek
Shake me, run me over,
And bring me to the top of the peak
Who am I, the one you should fall & wash His feet
The one, I hope you meet when you are deceased
Who am I, the spiritual essence
With the rock solid presence
I'm a child of God asking for a lesson
And His blessing
Who am I, a product of Imani
This is my confession
Love, Grace, and Imani 2005(edited)

Life's Lessons

Pretty faces, different places
People embracing, wine tasting
Different paths, different money,
Different math, Different occupation,
Different tasks, some down to earth,
Some too much class
Need to look into the glass
Before it drops & crashes
Life's days are slow; years are fast
Live for tomorrow not the past,
Today is here, every hour, every minute,
Every second, Life is the teacher.
Do we get the lesson?
Do we understand our blessing?
Where will we rest eternally?
New day, new life, times not so rough,
Plenty is enough, when you trust God
Real smiles, real laughs, no two paths,
Just one straight to the gates
This allowed through my faith
Imani will cleanse the soul;
Believe with all our hearts I was told
Now I can walk the streets of gold
When I get discouraged, I look at my gold
The engraving reminds me of my goal
Which is to protect my soul,
My life, my presence, my essence
Life's a journey that is the lesson
Love, Grace, and Imani 2005(edited)

My Time of Need

As I hold God's hand through my pain and hurt
Slowly He heals me, another one of His great works
Man is not here in my time of need
Jesus is, that is why He did bleed
Lord take care of me in my darkest night
Quickly but softly restore my might
When my head burns, hold my hand tight
To let me forget you're there for my fight
I pray this prayer because I believe in You
Faith, that there is nothing You won't and cannot do
You are here for me
Even though I fall short of Your glory
You know all my excuses and sad stories
Through it all you are here during my time of need
When I was hungry, You did feed
When I was dying of thirst, You did bleed
The wine is a symbol of Your blood You shed
I feel Your hand as I lay in my bed
This prayer I pray in Jesus' name
I know I'm the reason He came
Please forgive me of my sins, Amen
Love, Grace, and Imani 2005(edited)

Moments

On days, where I want to be left alone
I turn off the TV, DVD, and CD's;
I turn off my phone
I need that time to relax and kick back,
Bring everything back intact
I am living the truth of
What I feel no need to act
Writing verses, lines, or words that rhyme
Brings me joy, reminds me of the picture
When I rode a green machine
As boy, I was innocent
Not knowing the difficulty of this world,
This place, no bad times, no being sad
I was always positive,
Always a smile on my face
Now I pick and search for success,
On a mission to reach
The vision, or to prolong it
Or extend it till victory is done
That day will come,
Where I know it was a job well done
Then I will rest knowing
I made a way for the next to go
And keep these moments these times,
They will read these poems, these rhymes,
Words sounding new but still the same,
What was good is now better;
Locked in these pages is forever
Love, Grace, and Imani 2005(edited)

Him

Take a spin in my world like a chrome rim
So I show you the brightest to the dim
I will make you think twice about him
Laid back on the outside,
But he cries on the inside
His nature is cool, calm, collective; smooth
Without a care in his heart with nothing to lose
Laid back like a million dollar cruise
Smooth as Bally shoes
And with the twitch of an eye
Outside he shed a tear, I seen him cry
I saw his heart stop beating, yes I saw him die
I saw his smoothness untied
Honestly no lie
I saw his vulnerability
How do I know?
Because I am that guy
Love, Grace, and Imani 2005 (edited)

My Downfall, My Demise

On that night, you made me think
You made me wink, you made me sink,
As I look at you in pink
Your hair, your face, your smile, your cheeks,
It all made me weak
However I maintained, I stayed sane
I stayed clam
Even though you could have been in my palm
I like your cheer, your charm,
I like to picture you in my arm
Till Florida again I weather the storm
-to see your hips,
Listen to your mind, lay back,
And enjoy the bliss
Just look at the pictures…if you ever miss
Love, Grace, and Imani 2005

Send a Lady

I hustle love and a broken heart brings reality
Reduce calories sharpen my thoughts actually
The past is in the back of me, every moment,
Every time plays in my mind,
Now I understand every line
Raindrops mixed with sunshine, no second story;
this version is only mine
Summer blues are hard to accept
even when it is hot
So I think not of the effect of the butterfly
I close that chapter, that book, I said goodbye
No reason to wonder what is the truth,
what is lies
I am going to trade in my life
I believe I can fly,
however heaven I need a hug
I need a true love to stand
through the thick and thin
Feel like my kin, bring my new kin,
Where do I begin?
Conversations, let's be friends,
Heal my heart let it mend
Let the disappoint of the past end
Reflections of my soul are my feelings for real
I lived that life of love at a standstill
My prayer every other night
"Lord hold me through these hard times"
HE comforted my body, my mind, in due time
HE will send that lady of mine

Send a Lady continued…

That one who will cherish me
Like a soldier in Iraq
Just get here if you can,
I need you right by my side
Tomorrow is not promise,
So I need you to enjoy every moment,
This is life
She keeps everything intact,
She is the strength like Mama, she never lacks
A Christian lady that has my back
She will be God sent
To help this man love again
On my knees this prayer begins
Love, Grace, and Imani 2005 (edited)

Speak to my Heart

Speak to my heart Holy Spirit, correct my wrongs
Lord I pray come hold me in Your arms
Give me Your Holy Word to guide my soul
I am reaching my hands out please hold
I do not know what to do
Until YOU speak to my heart
I need Your help to heal what is apart
I should have talk to YOU from the start
YOU have always been my light
When it was dark, Lord correct my ways,
Make my temple at ease, Speak to my heart;
Give me Your Word so I can please
Lord correct my soul;
Save Your child, give me hope
Speak to my heart,
I'm drowning please throw me a rope
I need Your help,
Lord I'm ready for Sunday morning
It's been Your love I have been yearning
Keep on talking to my heart because I hear
Keep on talking to my heart and make it clear
Send those Angels
Let them comfort me with their wings
Speak to my heart as Donnie McClurkin sings
Bring the love to my heart, I'm ready
Lord, hug me and hold me steady,
Let Your Spirit guide, and let Your Word apply
Lord thank you,
For being my Savior and staying by my side
My prayer to the Highest of the most high
Love, Grace, and Imani 2005 (edited)

Gifts of Grace

Gifts of Grace,
Is when I got that new place
Gifts of Grace,
Is when I saw that smiling face
Gifts of Grace,
Is the sweet taste of victory
Gifts of Grace,
Is when the Holy Spirit enters me
Gifts of Grace
Help me to run this race
Gifts of Grace,
Is where sadness can be replaced
Gifts of Grace,
Got me to this moment, this hour
Gifts of Grace,
Got me to love, got me this power
Gifts of Grace
Brought me to be a man and tower
Gifts of Grace
Allows me to give constant thanks
Gifts of Grace,
Allow me to think positive
Gifts of Grace
Gives me the confidence for this direction
Gifts of Grace
Let me I know I was made in his image
And I will be great
Love, Grace, and Imani 2005 (edited)

Still Here

As I take time out to think how I felt a year ago
I was hurt, I felt alone, no one to call my own
Poems of about my heartache being written daily
No phone calls because no one is there to listen
Day by day that person I'm missing
No job, no check, I felt low like concrete
Hard to stay up beat
However, the kingdom I renewed and seek
Days of misery feeling like a week
Minutes feeling like hours
I felt like an X-man with no powers
I was an ex-man not involved in the new plan
But that's when I began to be the next man
The one that's going to make it one way or another
From the days I put plans in my mind
How they turned and mapped out on time
With Imani, the belief everything would be fine
He restored my riches now I'm waiting to overdose
I say cheers with Krug; I owe Him a toast
I will spread His words from coast to coast
Reflections of my soul, naked and afraid
I just took my course by force of dealing with truth
Never was catholic but I confessed daily in a booth
Really a book, some pages I never even looked
Just wrote about what it took, what it takes
Not ashamed to let them see the tears on my face
A year later this is still what I embrace
I'm here now, God carried me through my mistakes
I'm smiling for what's next as I patiently wait
Love, Grace, and Imani 2005 (edited)

1
The Mind, the Pen, the Paper
Reflections of the Soul
8

2005

Cover Concept & Design by Edward Thornton III
& Marcus Yates Ford

The Mind, the Pen, the Paper

As thoughts come from above the maintain
In my brain words start to rain
So instead of losing them
I grab a pen so they can retained.
Then comes the paper,
And a poem is obtained
It is the same process every time, simple and plain.
Wisdom transferred, and it is something I gain
This is how I become an entry maker
From the mind to the pen to the paper
The Mind, the Pen, the Paper 2005 (edited)

Wounds

Emotions...
Surround me in my place
Bullets flying at my back, the sides, my face
Ambush!
My brain cries, Emotions of protection I guide
Emotions from lack of security, I can't hide
My heart is hit from every angle, open and wide
Shell-shocked,
Wishing and holding on to life, not to die
Helicopter!
Ben Taub save me!
Let's fly!
Asking, *Why me, Lord Why?*
Wounds all over my body;
Holding on to my cross pendant, I survive
Resting in my bed, I'm well and alive
Back at the house laying in my bed
The moonlight comes through my window
Tears of mine begin to start
The description of this man with a broken heart
The Mind, the Pen, the Paper 2005 (edited)

Trouble Man

I'm a trouble man, with nothing to lose
I'm a trouble man, with nothing to choose
I'm a trouble man, who women refuse
I'm a trouble man, don't get it confused
I'm a trouble man, who is mental abused
I'm a trouble man, who is falsely accused

I'm a trouble man, who needs to pray
I'm a trouble man, what more can I say?
I'm a trouble man, no time to play
I'm a trouble man, lonely every day
I'm a trouble man, doing it my way
I'm a trouble man, I will stay

I'm a trouble man that even Jesus can save
The Mind, the Pen, the Paper 2005 (edited)

When I was Willing

When I was willing to be trusted,
You did not trust
When I was willing to make love,
You thought it was lust
When I was willing to make it we,
You thought of you
When I was willing to commit,
You would not compromise
When I was willing to tell truths,
You treated me as if they were lies
When I was willing to make you the one,
You questioned my intentions
When I was willing to talk,
You heard but did not listen.
When I was willing to analyze,
You did not want to ponder
When I was willing to plan,
You did not want to wonder

The Mind, the Pen, the Paper 2005 (edited)

Unstoppable

God takes us through paths to make us stronger.
You are almost there
It will not be much longer:
Keep your head to the sky and rise to the top.
During this time, you will be put to test:
With God's hand, this time will be breeze.
Remember to always relax
And keep your mind at ease:
Remember you are a child of God-
Everything is possible.
Pray and keep the Spirit and you are stoppable.
The Mind, the Pen, the Paper 2005 (edited)

You who kept me Strong

In my time of need,
Guide my heart not my thoughts
Please guide me to truth
And things that can't be bought
Touch me in my darkest nights:
Be my diamond and shine so bright light;
Clear my path so I can keep my sight
Our relationship no one understands but us;
Teach me again how to focus on love
Thank you for the oil to my heart
Thank you being with me from the start
Time after time you save me from harm;
When I am cold you still keep me warm
Please hold my hands, my arm
And let me step back to my charm
Stay with me,
Never leave my side, never be gone
It was you who kept my strong
The Mind, the Pen, the Paper 2005 (edited)

Where I'm From

As I reflect, where I'm from
Where God's Grace
Has allowed me to see the sun
Living with blessings, another day has begun
As I reflect, I thank Him where I'm from
The teachings and the hands that reach
The strength that helps me rise from defeat
The light in the dark when I can't see
Listening to all my prayers,
When I weep and I'm weak
As I reflect, where I'm from
All I did was ask for it to come
With the thirteenth letter and words
Came greatness with spiritual essence
With the sixth letter and words
Came my foundation
With the rock solid presence
It came piece by piece, struggles and victories
Thy will be done
I stand as a product of faith,
That is where I'm from
The Mind, the Pen, the Paper 2005 (edited)

Coin

Now sturdy and straight,
Do not get concerned with fate
Because you have to seek and never wait
As days press, my clothes still are not starched
I put my pants on, they are still apart
Walk toward the light, not the dark
Someone's ruins is another's treasure
Some never took the time to measure
We all out flipping coins in the well
Those quarters just stack and have a story to tell
Listen…Lost dreams
They really thought that coin could make it happen
Nickels and dimes under the water just laughing
Dreams continue to come and go;
However, dreams continue to create
Sometimes dreams do not occur
Because dreamers dream too late

The Mind, the Pen, the Paper 2005 (edited)

Coin... the afterthought

Never stop Dreaming
On the other hand,
Maybe the order of operations was misplaced
'And whatever things you ask in prayer,
Believing, you will receive"
This is where dreams are conceived
This is how dreams are achieved

Matthew 21:22

Symbol Design by
Edward Thornton III & Marcus Yates Ford

Create Inspire Enhance

Marcus Yates Ford
Missouri City, Texas

Signet Playlist
Chicago 12 for LC

Beginnings
Saturday in the Park
25 or 6 to 4
Hard Habit to Break
Street Player
Hard to Say I'm Sorry
Love Me Tomorrow
You're the Inspiration
Make Me Smile
Does Anybody Really Know What Time it is?
Take Me Back to Chicago
Alive Again

2012
Born and Raised Album
Song Number 10
Whiskey, Whiskey, Whiskey - John Mayer

Surrender Playlist
27: Praise Message Soul: Love

Jesus is Love - The Commodores
More than Anything - Sunday Service Choir
For Your Glory - Tasha Cobbs Leonard
I Look to You - Whitney Houston
There is More - Lexi
I'm Gonna Be Ready - Yolanda Adams
God is Blessing - Jonathan Nelson
God Favored Me - Hezekiah Walker
Oh How Precious - Kathy Taylor
Worth - Anthony Brown
A Great Work - Brian Courtney Wilson
It's Working - William Murphy
Won't He Do It - Koryn Hawthorne
We're Blessed - Fred Hammond
For the Rest of My Life - Rev Timothy Wright
I Believe - Marvin Sapp
No Other Name - Freddy Rodriguez
Every Praise - Hezekiah Walker
Speak to My Heart - Voice of Joy
I Shall Wear a Crown - Deleon
The Beauty of the Cross - Crystal Lewis
Fly like a Bird - Mariah Carey
My Name is Victory - Jonathan Nelson
Thank You - Mary Mary
Tomorrow - The Winans
Something About the Name Jesus - Kirk Franklin
Going Up Yonder - Larry Davis

Bonus
Hosanna - Kirk Franklin

Signature Thoughts

As you read my moments, my thoughts, my visions, my lessons, and my situations that make me who I am, hold on to whatever message attaches to your understanding and realize that this is my creativity who makes me who I am.

This is my written picture of words,
and like a painting, I allowed it to dry.

All of the material is a composition of the
past, the present & the unknown...
Some of these writings were simply how
I was feeling at a particular time.
This is my story in a creative form,
so, I can read it again.
We, as people, grow every day and have the
right to change our minds. Remember that
you can't just love one part of me;
it takes many parts to make one whole

Love is Easy
Let us not make it hard

Thank you for the love and support

www.ingramcontent.com/pod-product-compliance
Lightning Source LLC
Chambersburg PA
CBHW041620220426
43661CB00049B/1548